better together*

*This book is best read together, grownup and kid.

 akidsco.com

a
kids
book
about

a kids book about DISABILITY

by Kristine Napper

A Kids Co.
Editor Jelani Memory
Designer Duke Stebbins
Creative Director Rick DeLucco
Studio Manager Kenya Feldes
Sales Director Melanie Wilkins
Head of Books Jennifer Goldstein
CEO and Founder Jelani Memory

DK
Editor Emma Roberts
Senior Production Editor Jennifer Murray
Senior Production Controller Louise Minihane
Senior Acquisitions Editor Katy Flint
Managing Art Editor Vicky Short
Publishing Director Mark Searle
DK would like to thank Tony Stevens and Kamran Mallick

This American Edition, 2023
Published in the United States by DK Publishing
1745 Broadway, 20th Floor, New York, NY 10019

DK, a Division of Penguin Random House LLC
Text and design copyright © 2020 by A Kids Book About, Inc.
A Kids Book About, Kids Are Ready, and the colophon 'a' are trademarks of A Kids Book About, Inc.
23 24 25 26 27 10 9 8 7 6 5 4 3 2 1
001-336882-Aug/2023

A catalog record for this book is available from the Library of Congress.
ISBN: 978-0-7440-8568-6

DK books are available at special discounts when purchased in bulk for
sales promotions, premiums, fund-raising, or educational use. For details, contact:
DK Publishing Special Markets, 1745 Broadway, 20th Floor, New York, NY 10019, or SpecialSales@dk.com

Printed and bound in China

For the curious
www.dk.com

akidsco.com

MIX
Paper | Supporting
responsible forestry
FSC™ C018179

This book was made with Forest
Stewardship Council™ certified
paper—one small step in DK's
commitment to a sustainable future.
**For more information go to
www.dk.com/our-green-pledge**

To my parents, Karen and Ken, who have supported me through every dream, every whim, and every obstacle.

Intro
for grownups

Kids ask all kinds of questions about my wheelchair, but most frequently, grownups ask, "How should we talk about disability with kids?" They want the kids in their lives to be curious and informed as well as inclusive and accepting. These are great goals! But grownups are also afraid of saying the wrong thing or accidentally offending someone.

This book can be read with kids who have disabilities, know people with disabilities, or will meet disabled people out in the world—in other words, it's for everyone!

I can't answer all of your questions and I can't speak on behalf of all disabled people, but I can tell you about my own experience and help you start some conversations. It's OK if you don't know the answer to every question that might come up. Just talking about disability helps erase stigma.

So let's talk!

Hi, my name is Kristine.

If you could see me right now, you'd see...

brown hair with a little purple in the front,

some dangly earrings,

a cozy sweater,

and a pretty purple wheelchair.

(I call her Lydia.)

That's right, I have a **disability**.

I was born with **SMA**,
which stands for
Spinal **M**uscular **A**trophy.

It affects my whole body,
making my muscles weak.

While I can't stand up and walk around, *my chair goes really fast!*

Sometimes when people see
me and my chair...

they get uncomfortable,
they don't know what to say,
they talk to me like I don't understand,
they ask really personal questions,
they feel sorry for me,
and sometimes, they just
stare at me with a sad face.

Would you like people greeting you this way?

Not just once or twice, but *all the time*?

Probably not.

When they do this, it's not because
of my brown eyes,
or short hair,
and it's not because they're having a bad day.

It's because I have a disability.

Having a disability means you can't do something the way most people do, so you find a different way.

And there are even different
kinds of disabilities:

*physical, intellectual, emotional, learning,
behavioral, and so many more.*

I've learned a lot from living with a disability, so I'd like to share some things with you.

The **first** thing to know
about people with disabilities is ■ ■ ■ ■ ■ ■

 we are normal.

Yup, that's right.

We're not scary monsters, space aliens, or sad stories.

Normal people
come in all different
shapes,
sizes,
and colors.

Being normal means being different.

Having a disability is one of the MANY ways to be normal.

If you understand that disabled people are normal, then you'll have no problem with everything else we're going to talk about.

And guess what...

you're usually really good at this!

Sorry, grownups—you're usually not.

Kids are good at being curious and respectful, including people and not excluding them.

Grownups are usually just afraid they'll say or do the wrong thing.

So, because my disability is normal, how do you think I like to be treated?

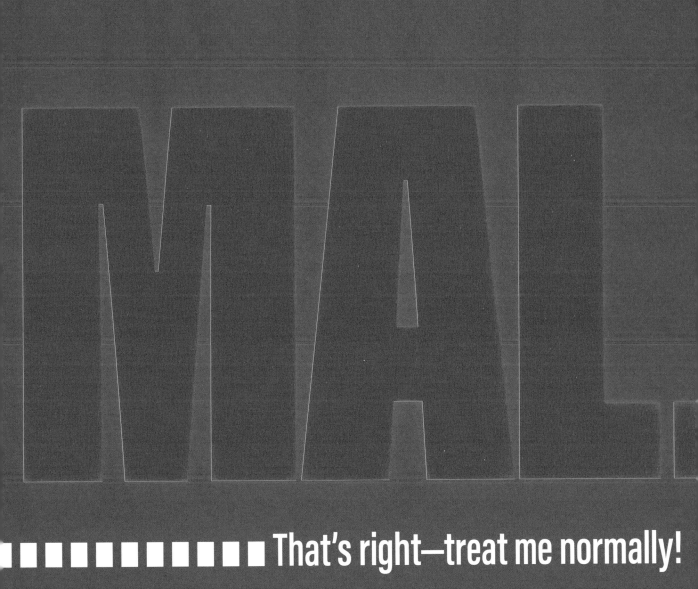

That's right—treat me normally!

You might wonder whether it's OK to help me. The answer is—sometimes.

There are lots of things I can do on my own, but some things I need help with.

I might ask for your help opening a door, reaching for something on the floor, or taking the cap off a marker.

If you think I might need help, it's OK to ask. I'll either say,

"*Yes, please!*" or, "*No, thank you.*"

But if I say no, please listen, because help I don't want really isn't helpful.

Another thing—I don't like being stared at. It's just not polite.

If you have a question about me,
my chair, or my disability, it's OK to ask.

Most of the time, it's totally OK!

But some questions aren't nice.
Some are kinda mean.
Questions like ■■■■■■■■■■■■■■■■■■■■■

"What's wrong with you?"

"How do you use the bathroom?"

"What happened to you?"

"Can you have babies?"

The best thing is to try to avoid questions that will make the other person feel bad or embarrassed.

So what do you talk about with
a person who has a disability?

ANYT

HING!

Ask,
"Hi, how are you?"
"How's your day going?"
Ask about what movies they like,
where they grew up,
or what their favorite ice cream flavor is.
(Mine is cookie dough!)

I love talking about my disability, but it's not the ONLY thing I want to talk about.

One last thing I want you to know
is—I am not broken.

I don't need to be fixed.

In fact, my disability helps me be a wiser, kinder, stronger person.

But, there is something really important that needs to change...

THE W

ORLD.

There are places I can't go
because nobody built a ramp or elevator.

I almost never see people with disabilities like mine on TV, in movies, or in books.

I have a job that I love. (I'm a teacher.)

But I know lots of disabled people who can't get jobs even though they *want* to work.

So,
try to notice
when people with disabilities are

left out, excluded, or

The world needs to be more *accessible*.

People need to be more *inclusive*.

Disabled people belong *everywhere*.

Outro
for grownups

I hope this book answered some questions. More importantly, I hope it inspires new questions! I didn't explain every big word or big idea introduced in this book—a book that long wouldn't fit on a shelf—but I hope you'll take the opportunity to dig deeper into anything that sparked curiosity. Kids and grownups can learn together about different disabilities, interesting people who have disabilities, and how to make the world more accessible.

As the kids in your life become comfortable with the different ways people navigate the world, you might be surprised by their brilliant ideas for improving accessibility. Their open minds and hearts might even help change the world. Thank you for starting the conversation!

About The Author

Kristine Napper (she/her) has used a wheelchair for as long as she can remember—in black, hot pink, shimmery blue, and now lavender purple. As a kid, Kristine managed to enjoy almost any activity she chose, thanks to her own creativity, and supportive friends and family.

When she grew up, moved out, went to college, and became a teacher, Kristine discovered many accessibility barriers in the grown-up world. She learned that those barriers were created by people, and they're fixable by people.

Kristine channels her creative, inclusive spirit into writing, teaching, and speaking. She believes our words can help people know better, and do better.

 @Kristine_Napper    @kristine.napper

Made to empower.

a kids book about racism
by Jelani Memory

a kids book about ANXIETY
by Ross Szabo

a kids book about DISABILITY
by Kristine Napper

a kids book about IMAGINATION
by LEVAR BURTON

a kids book about belonging
by Kevin Carroll
Bestselling Author of *Rules of the Red Rubber Ball*

a kids book about failure
by Dr. Laymon Hicks

a kids book about GRATITUDE
by Ben Kenyon

a kids book about LIFE ONLINE
by Dave S. Anderson & Blake Fleischacker

a kids book about body image
by Rebecca Alexander

a kids book about IMMIGRATION
by MJ Calderon
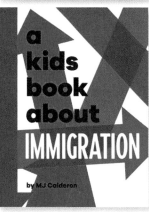

a kids book about EMPATHY
by Daron K. Roberts

a kids book about GENDER
by Dale Mueller

Discover more at akidsco.com